Foreword

The Lord also will be a refuge for the oppressed,
A refuge in times of trouble.
And those who know Your name will put their trust
    in You;
For You, Lord, have not forsaken those who seek
    You.

Psalm 9:9-10

In my heart of hearts, there is a glass-smooth pond set in a landscape of woods and fields, and every breeze and every earth tremor that ripples the surface of my still waters alerts me to pay close attention to the posture of my heart, the pitch and yaw of how I lean toward Christ. In these days, these last days, as the sky darkens, there is coming a storm of unimaginable proportions; the economic sky will turn black and the moral winds will howl as everything around us is tested to its limits. Many will lose heart, and many who draw close to Jesus will find breath, strength, and life. There are rudimentary things we must practice, not in dogmatic rhythm, but in the determined rhyme of heaven's song, the song heard in the fast-approaching footsteps of the coming King. He is coming!

Dan's book *Standing Firm in a Time of Shaking* outlines for us a scriptural path to follow to assure ourselves of the firmness of our steps toward our destiny in Christ. These are not just "things to do" as in some corporate production schedule measuring performance, but more the "things to do" that are participant to God's plan for our destiny, salvation, hope, and peace. Also, ultimately, we should practice these things, as seen in the pages of this book, in order to give God the glory that is solely His and His alone, that the Lamb would have the reward of His suffering. In *Standing Firm in a Time of Shaking*, you have a wonderful treat in store. May God bless you as you find stability and strength to continue on in the days to come.

—W.C. Whitaker

TABLE OF CONTENTS

Chapter 1

UNDERSTANDING THE TIME

We are living in a time when everything that can be shaken is being shaken. For example, in 1989, the Berlin Wall, which had long divided Germany, came down. A wall that had stood as an immovable fortress since 1961 was no more. For many years, the Soviet Union said, "There is no God." In December 1991, God shook and there was no Soviet Union! When much of the world was celebrating Christmas, the birth of the Son of God, the empire that had refused to acknowledge Him unraveled and was no more! At that time, much of Europe came out from under the iron fist of communism. Man may take the credit, and God uses people, but it was God who shook, and these seemingly immovable fortresses collapsed.

Going back in time further, we see the rebirth of the state of Israel in 1948, and the demonic activity operating through men who have tried to destroy and are still trying to destroy the very existence of Israel. In much more recent history, we see the removal of Saddam Hussein from power and the shaking of an oppressive centuries-old way of life in the whole Middle Eastern region, where a few have lorded it over the many, and women have been treated as second-class citizens and much worse.

Change is in the air all over the world, and in the words of a popular old song, **"There's a whole lotta shaking going on!"** There is also shaking in other areas, such as the U.S. economy. Oil prices continue to remain high as turmoil and instability in the Middle East continue and as nations such as China grow in industrial might and the worldwide demand for oil increases. The U.S. automobile industry has taken a beating from Japanese and other companies that produce more economical cars. In this nation, two of the major and historically unshakable carmakers, General Motors and Ford, have suffered severe setbacks in their fortunes.

The home mortgage industry and housing market have experienced a major shaking. Job security has suffered as manufacturing jobs have gone overseas, and many can no longer depend on working for the same firm all their lives and retiring with financial security. Nothing stays the same, and that is certainly true of the global economic picture. The rising economies of China, the EEC, and India are all changing the global economic picture. Here in the U.S. we continue to live in increasing debt as a nation. I firmly believe that it is only a matter of time before a severe economic storm shakes this country.

Even weather patterns have been shaken up in different parts of the world. In 2005, we had the most active hurricane season ever, with more named storms than any previous season on record. It included the catastrophic Hurricane Katrina. In the previous year, an enormous tsunami rose up out of the Indian Ocean without warning. The loss of life and devastation to the South Asian region was catastrophic, and the whole world gasped at the magnitude of the disaster.

What Is Going On?

The Pharisees and Sadducees asked Jesus for a sign, and part of His response is given in Matthew 16:2-3:

He answered and said to them, "When it is evening you say, 'It will be fair weather, for the sky is red'; and in the morning, 'It will be foul weather today, for the sky is red and threatening.' Hypocrites! You know how to discern the face of the sky, but you cannot discern the signs of the times."

As believers, we need to look at what is going on through spiritual eyes and discern the time we are living in from a spiritual perspective. We want a biblical perspective, not simply a natural perspective, or we will be in the dark like those who do not know the Lord. The Bible accurately describes this season in Hebrews 12:25-29:

See that you do not refuse Him who speaks. For if they did not escape who refused Him who spoke on earth, much more shall we not escape if we turn away from Him who speaks from heaven, whose voice then shook the earth; but now He has promised, saying, "Yet once more I shake not only the earth, but also heaven." Now this, "Yet once more," indicates the removal of those things that are being shaken, as of things that are made, that the things which cannot be shaken may remain. Therefore, since we are receiving a kingdom which cannot be shaken, let us have grace, by which we may serve God acceptably with reverence and godly fear. For our God is a consuming fire.

I do not pretend to know all that God is doing in the earth in these days, but one of the major things taking place is shaking! **God is preparing the earth for the return of the King and the full manifestation of His unshakable kingdom.** Between now and then, everything that is not of His kingdom is being or will be shaken!

Some Specifics Happening in This Time

- God is increasingly moving in the world. Revival has taken place or is taking place in different parts of the world, and I believe that revival is coming like a flood to this nation. Shaking is needed to usher in revival. As long as man feels secure in his self-sufficiency and independence from God, he will see little need to turn to God. We see how far from God this nation has drifted over the years, and the majority of people are living as if there is no God. Independence from God is what manifested in the Garden of Eden and caused man to fall, and that same independence is prevalent in much of society today. God is bringing unsaved man to the realization that he needs God!

- God wants to get the attention of His church. Much of the church in this nation has fallen asleep like the foolish virgins in one of Jesus' parables. It is time for us to wake up and get ready before it is too late. Just as God sent a storm to wake up Jonah when he was going the wrong way and avoiding his calling, **God has to shake the church or allow the church to be shaken that she may respond to her true calling and once again be on fire for Jesus!** "And do this, knowing the time, that now it is high time to awake out of sleep; for now our salvation is nearer than when we first believed. The night is far spent, the day is at hand. Therefore let us cast off the works of darkness, and let us put on the armor of light" (Romans 13:11-12).

- As the Lord has stepped up His activity in the earth, the evil one has stepped up his works of evil. "The thief does not come except to steal, and to kill, and to destroy" (John 10:10a). The dramatic rise of terrorism in recent years is evidence of the rise in the activities of the kingdom of darkness. The Bible also

12

says, "Therefore rejoice, O heavens, and you who dwell in them! Woe to the inhabitants of the earth and the sea! For the devil has come down to you, having great wrath, because he knows that he has a short time" (Revelation 12:12). We are on a time line to the end of this age and the beginning of the next.

The Purpose of This Book

The purpose of this book is to open our eyes and awaken us to the season we are living in. Its purpose is also to provide some biblical guidelines to help us stand firm so that we can make it through this time in victory. Many years ago, the Lord gave me the following word: "There is a time coming when many will run this way and that, not knowing where to turn, and they will look to those who know the Lord."

We are now in that time! The Lord wants to use each one of us as a beacon of light shining brightly in the darkness and pointing others to the One who is our security, the Lord Jesus Christ. **May the Lord encourage you and make you a fearless warrior who stands firm in Him in this time.**

Chapter 2

A KINGDOM THAT CANNOT BE SHAKEN

> Therefore, since we are receiving a kingdom which cannot be shaken, let us have grace, by which we may serve God acceptably with reverence and godly fear.

> Hebrews 12:28

When we are born again, whether we realize it or not at the time, we are taken out of one kingdom and moved immediately into another kingdom. We were subjects of the evil one and the kingdom of darkness; now we are set free from his rule and become subjects of Jesus our Lord, the King of the kingdom of God, the kingdom of light.

"He has delivered us from the power of darkness and conveyed us into the kingdom of the Son of His love, in whom we have redemption through His blood, the forgiveness of sins" (Colossians 1:13-14). This kingdom to which we now belong is unshakable and eternal. Our spirits are now alive and joined to the Spirit of God. **We are indeed new creations!**

However, having spent all of our lives up to this point in the dark kingdom, much of our way of thinking and many of our attitudes are those of the old kingdom. As a result, we feel very insecure when the world around us starts to shake, rattle, and roll! Our whole soul realm—mind, will, and emotions—still needs to be renewed so that it will conform to the attitudes and mind-set of the kingdom of God. The more we become like Christ, the less we will be shaken by what is going on in the world around us. It is God's desire to make us valiant soldiers in His army who will remain firm in faith and steady when everyone around us is losing it!

The Kingdom Within Us

Not only have we been transplanted into a new kingdom, but that new kingdom is planted on the inside of us as a seed. Jesus described the kingdom in Luke 17:20-21:

> Now when He was asked by the Pharisees when the kingdom of God would come, He answered them and said, "The kingdom of God does not come with observation; nor will they say, 'See here!' or 'See there!' For indeed the kingdom of God is within you."

As that seed is watered and nourished, it grows and starts to be revealed in our lives, where it can be seen by the world around us. It is a kingdom that begins on the inside and works its way to the outside, where the fruit, or results, of it can be seen. In a nutshell, the more we become like Christ on the inside, the more His life and the more His kingdom is manifested in and through our lives. It is a kingdom that has its source in the unseen, eternal, and unshakable God and His Word. "By faith we understand that the worlds were framed by the word of God, so that the things which are seen were not made of things which are visible" (Hebrews 11:3).

16

The Bible also says, "For the kingdom of God is not eating and drinking, but righteousness and peace and joy in the Holy Spirit" (Romans 14:17). The more like Christ we become, the more we will manifest righteousness, peace, and joy in a world that is coming apart at the seams! And the more our confidence rests in the Lord and His Word and the fact that we are members of an eternal kingdom that cannot be shaken, the more secure we will feel in an increasingly insecure world. **That is not only a wonderful thing for us, but is a shining testimony to unbelievers whose worlds are falling apart!**

Kingdom Provision

> But seek first the kingdom of God and His righteousness, and all these things shall be added to you.
> Matthew 6:33

There is no shortage of supply in God's kingdom. Our own personal kingdoms, the kingdom of the company we work for, and the kingdom of the country we live in are all subject to economic changes. I believe that this will be increasingly true in the future as God shakes or allows to be shaken all that man has created. If your source is your own personal finances, or your job, or the fortunes of the nation you live in, you will be severely shaken in the times we are living in.

For us who are believers, there is another option. If we will truly seek first the kingdom of God and His righteousness, God promises to supply all of our needs. From where will He supply them? The Bible says, "And my God shall supply all your need according to His riches in glory by Christ Jesus" (Philippians 4:19). The source is His riches in glory, or, in other words, His kingdom! He often will supply through man, but He is not limited by what man does or does not have. He fed the nation of Israel in the desert for forty years when there was no natural provision available!

We often have too small a picture of what God can do, and we make the mistake of thinking that we can figure out how He is going to provide. We can't! How He does it is His department. Our responsibility is to satisfy the conditions, namely to seek first His kingdom and not our own, and to seek first His righteousness, not our own. We have to repent of our natural tendency to build our own empires, and make ourselves available for the work of His kingdom. We also have to repent of all self-righteousness and allow God to work in our lives to make us more and more like Christ so that we manifest His righteousness. The conditions are tough, but if we satisfy them, we can know a peace and a security concerning our needs and the needs of our households in the days ahead, regardless of how uncertain the economic climate in which we live. **That is good news!**

Chapter 3

ABIDING IN THE UNSHAKABLE KING JESUS

Abide in Me, and I in you. As the branch cannot bear fruit of itself, unless it abides in the vine, neither can you unless you abide in Me.

John 15:4

Jesus is the unshakable King of the unshakable kingdom. Before a person is born again, he or she does not know Him and is not yet one of His friends or one of His subjects. In fact, like it or not, an unbeliever is a subject of the kingdom of darkness and lives under the tyrannical rule of its prince. Clearly, the most important thing for any unbeliever is to come to Jesus and receive Him as both Savior and Lord. What is the most important thing for a believer? There are several very good answers to this, but I believe that the best answer is to make his or her relationship with Him the TOP priority! If we examine John 15:1-17 unhurriedly, we will see that this is true. Not only is He the Source of our salvation, but He is also the Source of our lives after this. **We are not only to come to Him; we are to remain in Him.**

As a young believer, I was enthusiastic to do things for God, to do exploits. The Bible does say, "The people who know their God shall be strong, and carry out great exploits" (Daniel 11:32). However, I was jumping over the part about knowing God, and concentrating on doing exploits. It is good to be enthusiastic about what God has called one to do, but let us not put the cart before the horse. In John 15, Jesus uses the word "abide" or it's equivalent ten times in the first ten verses. "Abide" means to stay, remain, continue, dwell, or live. It is clear from this passage that He wants our focus to be on relationship with Him, first and foremost. It is easy to get caught up in straining and striving to be a fruitful Christian, but there is a much more restful and productive way.

If we develop a habit of abiding in Jesus, we will become increasingly fruitful in time. In John 15:2, we are told that if we are fruitful, God will prune our lives to make us more fruitful. If we continue to abide in Him, the promise is that we will bear much fruit (vs. 5, vs. 8), and finally fruit that remains (vs. 16). **If we will simply abide in Him, He will make us fruitful! The fruit that we produce will not be the fruit of self-effort, but fruit that is produced supernaturally naturally out of our relationship with Him.** It is fruit that will have His life in it and that will produce His life in others. It is so simple that most of us miss it! The Lord had to bring me back to this truth many times before it finally began to sink in!

Our ability to stand firm and be strong in this time depends directly on the strength of our union with Christ. "As you therefore have received Christ Jesus the Lord, so walk in Him, rooted and built up in Him and established in the faith, as you have been taught, abounding in it with thanksgiving" (Colossians 2:6-7). The very foundation of our lives as believers is rooted in and built on our relationship with Jesus. A shallow relationship means shallow roots that cannot survive a strong storm, and as the storms increase in the world around us, our roots in Jesus need to be deeper and stronger, and our relationship with Him more intimate. **A casual and superficial approach to our relationship with the Lord is nothing short of disastrous in this day in which we live! Our ability to endure to the end in this time is dependent on the extent to which we are truly abiding in Him.**

A Place of Peace and Security

> The Lord is my rock and my fortress and my
>   deliverer;
> My God, my strength, in whom I will trust;
> My shield and the horn of my salvation, my
>   stronghold.
>
>   Psalm 18:2

Is there a place of lasting peace and security in an increasingly insecure world? I do not believe that there will be lasting peace on earth until the Prince of Peace returns. However, there is a place of peace and security available to the believer, as the above passage makes clear. Psalm 91:1 goes on to say, "He who dwells in the secret place of the Most High shall abide under the shadow of the Almighty." The secret place of the Most High is our personal, private, and intimate relationship with the Lord Himself. When we live daily in that place of closeness to and intimacy with Him, we are under His shadow. In other words, we are under His complete protection. **It is because of and only because of our relationship with Him that we have the tremendous promise of His protection given here.** And the relationship described here is not a superficial one, but a very personal and intimate one. This promise is given again later in the same Psalm.

Because he has set his love upon Me, therefore I will
    deliver him;
I will set him on high, because he has known My
    name.
He shall call upon Me, and I will answer him;
I will be with him in trouble;
I will deliver him and honor him.

Psalm 91:14-15

If we feel insecure in the world as it is today, that is
perfectly understandable. However, the solution is not to
look for more security in our job, or in making more money,
or in moving to another place, or in changing our circumstances in some way. Some changes may be helpful, but in
themselves, they cannot give us the real and lasting security
that we need. That security can only be found in Him and in
a close and personal relationship with Him. The Scriptures
repeat this in another way.

I will lift up my eyes to the hills—
From whence comes my help?
My help comes from the Lord,
Who made heaven and earth.

Psalm 121:1-2

The psalmist starts by lifting up his eyes to the hills to
see if his help will somehow come from them, but then he
realizes that his help does not come from anything he can see
with his natural eyes, but from the Lord who created all he
can see. When we look to created things, natural things, as
the basis of our safety, we are barking up the wrong tree! The
Lord who created all these things is the only true Source of
the security we are seeking. It cannot be found in an impersonal academic knowledge about Him, but in knowing Him
personally and intimately. **No matter how good our rela-**

22

tionship with the Lord has been in the past, I believe that we need a deeper and closer and more intimate one in the day in which we are living!

Chapter 4

THE UNSHAKABLE WORD

If you abide in Me, and My words abide in you, you
will ask what you desire, and it shall be done for
you.

John 15:7

A close personal relationship with Jesus and a love for His
Word go together. If we try to relate to Jesus without
a regular feed on His Word, we get away from the Jesus of
the Bible and come up with our own ideas about who Jesus
is. This will lead us into deception, as we will tailor our
picture of Him to suit our own lifestyles and desires. We will
wind up going our own way and doing our own thing while
deceiving ourselves that we are walking with Him! And if
we focus purely on the written Word, without majoring in
an intimate daily walk with Jesus, the living Word, we wind
up living by an impersonal set of principles. Good principles, to be sure, but just as the Pharisees did, we will become
religious people without a personal and intimate relationship
with Jesus Christ. Without a living, growing daily walk with
Him, we have missed the heart of the Christian life! We may
become theologically correct people, but our love for Him
and others will grow cold, and our hearts will be far from

25

Him. **Living in relationship with Jesus and having His words live in us are inseparable.**

There is also more to having His words live in us than simply having an intellectual understanding of them. Just as Jesus became the Word made flesh, His words are to be made flesh in us. We are not only meant to read and feed on the Word of God, but we are meant to let it transform us so that we become more and more like Jesus. Our lives should be undergoing continual change, becoming less and less like the old person we used to be and more and more like Him! Ask someone who knows you well enough to be honest with you whether you are more like Christ than you were a year ago. The change may be gradual, but it should be happening!

Absorbing the Word of God

> This Book of the Law shall not depart from your mouth, but you shall meditate in it day and night, that you may observe to do according to all that is written in it. For then you will make your way prosperous, and then you will have good success.
>
> Joshua 1:8

This passage contains a prescription for getting the Word of God to live and remain in us. I believe that in the context of the new covenant, we can take the book of the law to be the whole Bible—the Word of God. This prescription gets the Word into our mouths, into our hearts and minds as we meditate on it, and all the way down to our feet as we do it. **When our mouths say it, and our hearts and minds believe it, and our feet walk in it, then surely the Word of God is abiding—living—in us!**

The Bible feeds our spirits, renews our minds, and even benefits the health of our bodies.

When facing one of the devil's temptations, Jesus said, "It is written, 'Man shall not live by bread alone, but by every word of God'" (Luke 4:4). How strong would you and me be physically if we had one meal a week? Not very! It is amazing how many of us expect to be spiritually strong and on top of our game on one feed of the Bible a week! Once we are born again, our spirits require spiritual food. I believe that many of us try to satisfy our spiritual hunger with more food, more excitement, more of something natural without even realizing it. I believe that if we would have a regular intake of spiritual nourishment, it would go a long way toward restoring our lives to a healthy and normal balance in other areas.

Ephesians 4:23 says, "Be renewed in the spirit of your mind," and Romans 12:2 says, "Do not be conformed to this world, but be transformed by the renewing of your mind, that you may prove what is that good and acceptable and perfect will of God."

The Holy Spirit and the Word of God work together to renew the way we think. Our minds are constantly barraged by the world around us, through television, radio, ads, etc., and by the unbelievers around us. The world is loudly trying to sell us its values, ideas, and lusts. What chance do our minds have without a regular intake of the Word of God? Not much! We need to actively decide what diet to feed our minds because if we don't decide, the world around us will do it for us.

A Beneficial Effect on Our Health

My son, give attention to my words; incline your ear to my saying. Do not let them depart from your eyes; keep them in the midst of your heart; for they are life to those who find them, and health to all their flesh.

Proverbs 4:20-22

I have a video of Derek Prince's testimony, given many years ago. In it he shares a real life experience of the healing effect of the Word of God. He was in a medical corps, stationed in North Africa during the Second World War. In that dry and hot climate, he contracted a skin condition that was incurable in that climate. It occurred to him that medication often is taken three times a day after meals. So he decided to read the Bible three times a day after his meals. In about four months, he was totally healed!

Building on a Firm Foundation

> But why do you call Me 'Lord, Lord,' and not do the things which I say? Whoever comes to Me, and hears My sayings and does them, I will show you whom he is like: He is like a man building a house, who dug deep and laid the foundation on the rock. And when the flood arose, the stream beat vehemently against that house, and could not shake it, for it was founded on the rock. But he who heard and did nothing is like a man who built a house on the earth without a foundation, against which the stream beat vehemently; and immediately it fell. And the ruin of that house was great.
>
> Luke 6:46-49

The Lord makes a clear distinction between those who pay Him lip service only, calling Him Lord, and those who genuinely obey Him. The one who hears and obeys is pictured as a house—a life—built on an unshakable foundation. But the one who hears but does not follow through with a life of obedience is pictured as a house—a life—built on sand.

Notice that Jesus does not say IF, but WHEN the flood comes. The flood represents those trials, storms, and times of adversity that come to test our faith and to try the foundation of our lives. Whether we stand or not depends to a large degree on our obedience level to the Lord. **It is not only knowing what the Bible says that makes us strong, but also doing it!** When the sun is shining and the sky is blue and everything is going well, even a foundation of sand will seem firm. However, when the going gets tough, the true nature of our foundation will be revealed.

Jesus said, "Heaven and earth will pass away, but My words will by no means pass away" (Matthew 24:35).

Chapter 5

THESE ARE THE DAYS OF THE EXTRA OIL

Then the kingdom of heaven shall be likened to ten virgins who took their lamps and went out to meet the bridegroom. Now five of them were wise, and five were foolish. Those who were foolish took their lamps and took no oil with them, but the wise took oil in their vessels with their lamps. But while the bridegroom was delayed, they all slumbered and slept. And at midnight a cry was heard: 'Behold the bridegroom is coming; go out to meet him!' Then all the virgins arose and trimmed their lamps. And the foolish said to the wise, 'Give us some of your oil, for our lamps are going out.' But the wise answered, saying, 'No, lest there should not be enough for us and you; but go rather to those who sell, and buy for yourselves.' And while they went to buy, the bridegroom came, and those who were ready went in with him to the wedding; and the door was shut.

Matthew 25:1-10

This passage describes two kinds of believers that would be found prior to His return: wise virgins and foolish virgins. Oil in the Bible is a picture of the Holy Spirit. The foolish virgins relied on their initial experience of the Holy Spirit to enable them to last the distance. However, the race that we are called to run is not a one hundred-yard dash, but a long-distance marathon. Jesus said, "And you will be hated by all for My name's sake. But he who endures to the end will be saved" (Matthew 10:22). No matter how well we begin the race, we need to be able to finish it!

I had a wonderful conversion experience as a teenager. My life was turned completely around, and I felt like I was walking a few feet above the ground for about six months. However, as time passed, I slowly started to run dry. I tried to bolster up my walk with good intentions and human enthusiasm and will power, but none of that worked for any length of time. I tried to do the right things that a Christian was supposed to do, but discovered that my own strength and determination were just not enough. **I needed extra oil!**

The wise virgins had the mentality of long-distance runners. They realized that they were in this race for the long haul and that they would need extra oil to last the distance. They had an eternal perspective, rather than a temporal, or short-term, perspective. Another interesting thing about this parable is that the bridegroom came at midnight. Midnight represents a time of intense darkness, and it describes how things will be in the world when Jesus returns. We are certainly living in a time when the darkness in the world around us is getting steadily darker. **Not only is extra oil needed to last the distance, but it also is needed to be able to continue the race in an increasingly tough time!**

How Do We Get Extra Oil?

As a young believer who needed extra oil but did not know how to get it, I gradually gave up and gradually slid back into the world. I knew that Jesus was real, but did not know how to stay in the Christian race. Many years later, the Lord drew me back to Himself and led me step by step to the

place of coming into more of His Spirit. **To receive more
of the Lord, one has to be hungry—really hungry—for
more! Then one has to ask.** The Bible says, "Blessed are
those who hunger and thirst for righteousness, for they shall
be filled" (Matthew 5:6).

I was really hungry for more, but was unfamiliar with
what I was hearing concerning being filled with the Spirit.
I had been born again and did not really know if there was
more. I also did not understand what speaking in tongues
was all about. I tried reading a little on the subject, but it
only got me all the more confused. So one day, I just came
to the Lord in simplicity and prayed, as best I can remember,
"Lord, if there is more, then please give me more. I receive
it by faith." That evening, I began to experience the begin-
nings of a new boldness in my life. A few days later, my
mouth began to tremble when having a quiet time, and a
while later, I realized that I should supply some sound. That
was the beginning of my speaking in tongues!

The Lord deals with each of us as individuals so that
the specific way that each of us comes into more of Him
may be different. Sometimes other believers around us try
to put God in a box and insist we experience Him just like
they did. **Don't put God in a box, and don't let others put
God in a box for you. God is bigger than all our boxes!**
Simply come to Him and tell Him that you need more of
Him. Let Him meet you where you are, as one of His unique
and beloved children.

We Need to Stay Filled

The Bible exhorts us in Ephesians 5:18 to "be filled with
the Spirit." The meaning is to keep on being filled so that
once we are filled and empowered to live the Christian life,
we continue being filled. Imagine a bucket with holes in
it. After it has been filled, water will leak out of it until it is
empty. That is like a Christian who is relying on his or her

relationship with the Lord of many years ago, but who is not actively and daily abiding in the Lord and walking with Him in the present. It is good to remember our experiences of God in the past, but it is not good to live in the past! If we want to stay filled, we need to maintain our daily walk with the One who is the Source of our new life.

Most of us would believe that Peter and John, who had experienced being filled with the Spirit at Pentecost, would surely not need to be filled again! However, when we read Acts 4, we find something very interesting. Peter and John were arrested and brought before the Jewish authorities for preaching, and they were commanded not to speak or teach in the name of Jesus. After that incident, they were released and went back to their companions to tell them what had happened. They had a prayer meeting and prayed for boldness.

> And when they had prayed, the place where they were assembled together was shaken; and they were all filled with the Holy Spirit, and they spoke the word of God with boldness.
>
> Acts 4:31

If Peter and John needed a fresh infilling of the Holy Spirit, we most certainly will need fresh infillings in our lives! It is impossible to live a consistent or victorious Christian life in our own strength or wisdom. I tried as a young man and failed. Many better people than me have tried and failed. **Jesus sent us the Promise of the Father—the Holy Spirit—to enable us to make it!** If you have never been filled with the Spirit, or are not sure whether you have been or not, simply go to Jesus and ask Him humbly. He is the Baptizer in the Holy Spirit (Luke 3:16). If you have been filled, you can ask Him regularly to fill you full to overflowing again!

Chapter 6

THE UNSHAKABLE FATHER

We repeat, we really saw and heard what we are now
writing to you about. We want you to be with us in
this—in this fellowship with the Father, and Jesus
Christ his Son.

1 John 1:3 (J.B. Phillips)

I grew up in a home where both of my parents were Christians and were very good parents. They were not perfect,
nor have I been a perfect parent. But I always knew that
they loved me, even when I blew it. This happened a lot in
my late teenage years and early twenties! I was saved in my
early teens, and Jesus became real to me. I drifted away over
a period of time and lived as a prodigal for many years, but
even during that time, I still knew that Jesus was real. At age
twenty-eight, He graciously brought me back to Himself and
restored me. However, because I had a good earthly father
who did not reject me even when I was a prodigal, I never
really felt the need to relate in a close and intimate way to
my heavenly Father. Many believers like me have come to
Jesus and developed a close relationship with Him but have
not gone on to have a close and intimate one with Father
God as well.

In 1996, my dad went to be with the Lord, and that left a big hole in my life. He and my mother were living in Australia at the time, and we were living in the United States, but we had kept in touch regularly by mail and by phone. When my earthly father was no longer available, I felt insecure on the inside, as I had no father to relate to! I had a good relationship with Jesus as my Lord, Savior, and best Friend, a great wife and two children, and my mother was still alive, but there came into my life a void that could only be filled by a father. And I lived with that void, not really realizing how big it was. With that void came an inner sense of insecurity, which would surface during times of stress and tiredness. **We are designed to have a relationship with both the Father and the Son.**

My first breakthrough came during the spring of 2005, when my wife and I were in a meeting where the praise and worship was truly awesome. During that time, I had a vision of standing under a night sky that was overcast. There was a circular hole in the clouds above me, and I was standing in a circle of light that was shining down on me. Darkness was all around. And the Lord said, "This is one of My beloved sons in whom I am well pleased." I just broke down and wept and did not care who saw me. I just began to realize that I had a heavenly Father who loved me and valued me and cared about me. Over that summer, my wife and I attended two conferences given by Jack Frost and Shiloh Place Ministries. The theme was "Restoring the Father's Love." The result was life changing for me. I had spent most of my Christian life knowing that Jesus loved me, and fellowshipping with Him, but not knowing the Father experientially in the sense of walking in His love and fellowshipping with Him. Now that has begun to change!

Restoration to the Father

> Jesus said to him, "I am the way, the truth, and the life.
> No one comes to the Father except through Me."
>
> John 14:6

Although this passage has rightly been used as an evangelistic passage, there is more to it than that. Jesus came not only to save us from the power and consequences of sin, but also to restore us to a relationship with the Father **in this life** as well as the next. Many believers have stopped at salvation and relationship with Jesus without coming into a real and intimate relationship with the Father. In doing so, we are still saved, but we are missing out on experiencing the fullness of Jesus' purpose in coming! He came that we might be restored into the relationship with the Father that Adam had before the fall. After the fall, Adam lost that Father-son relationship with God, and he and the human race after him were effectively orphaned. **Jesus came to restore that Father-son relationship to man.** Incidentally, the term "son" includes men and women when referring to a child of God. **Whether you are a son or daughter in the natural, you are a spiritual and eternal son of Father God if you are in Christ!** "For you are all sons of God through faith in Christ Jesus. For as many of you as were baptized into Christ have put on Christ. There is neither Jew nor Greek, there is neither slave nor free, there is neither male nor female; for you are all one in Christ Jesus" (Galatians 3:26-28).

An Orphan or a Son?

To this day, those outside Christ lives as orphans, and regrettably many believers live the same way. In Matthew 6, the Bible gives a clear description of the difference between living in a Father-son relationship with God and living as an orphan. Only two verses are quoted here, but reading the passage from verse 25 to the end of the chapter gives a more complete picture.

> Therefore do not worry, saying, "What shall we eat?" or "What shall we drink?" or "What shall we wear?" For after all these things the Gentiles seek. For your heavenly Father knows that you need all these things.
>
> Matthew 6:31-32

Gentiles here represent those living outside Christ. If we are living in Christ, whether of Jewish or Gentile descent in the natural, we belong to the people of God and are members of His household. This passage shows that those who do not know the Lord, who do not have a relationship with the Father, have no Father to take care of them. They live like orphans who have to take care of themselves. They have to worry, fight, and compete for everything that they have! As believers, we have no need to live like that. We have a heavenly Father who is well able to take care of us and provide for us. We are to trust Him and to trust His love for us, and are not to be anxious and afraid, fighting others in a dog-eat-dog way to get our needs met. We are not orphans anymore and don't need to live like them. The next verse goes on to explain how we are to live in His provision.

> But seek first the kingdom of God and His righteousness, and all these things shall be added to you.
>
> Matthew 6:33

If we live the way described in this verse, we are free to love others because we are now walking in the Father's loving care and provision for us. It is a daily walk of simple faith and obedience and fellowship with Him, where we put Him first and do what He says, and He takes care of us. We are His dependants! **This is radically different from the way of this orphan world.** God wants us to be channels of His love and blessing to others and in this way to reveal the Father and Jesus to them. If we live in a competitive, aggressive, faithless way, all the time trying to get our own way and fighting to get our needs met, how will they see the Lord in us? I believe that the more we get to know the Father, the more free we will be to simply love others without seeing them as threats and without trying to control, manipulate, and use them to get our own needs met. They will see in us the genuine thing, and we will be witnesses without trying to be! We also will come to know more peace and security in our own lives as we learn to look to our Father who loves us to provide for us, instead of looking to ourselves or others as the source of our provision.

A True Picture of the Father

> Jesus said to him, "Have I been with you so long, and yet you have not known Me, Philip? He who has seen Me has seen the Father; so how can you say, 'Show us the Father?'"
>
> John 14:9

What is the Father really like? If you have grown up with a father who was harsh and unkind, or cruel and abusive, you may feel that if that is what a father is like, you want nothing to do with Father God. We live in a fallen world, and many—especially in this day and age—have had bad father experiences or even no father experience. The thought of having a close relationship with Father God can be scary! Not only that, but religion has tended to present a picture of Father God as angry, judgmental, having a big stick, and ready to jump on us with both feet the moment we slip up! It is small wonder that many who come to Jesus still tend to shy away from getting close to Father God. **Father God is like none of these false pictures! Father God is exactly like Jesus!**

Jesus Himself said that if we have seen Him, we have seen the Father. In Hebrews 1:1-3, the Bible explains how God, meaning God the Father, revealed Himself in various ways in the time before Christ came, but now has revealed Himself fully in Christ. In verse 3, Jesus is described as "the brightness of His glory and the express image of His person." I encourage you to read the whole passage. What is clear is that **Father God is EXACTLY like Jesus!**

- Jesus is loving and kind. Father God is loving and kind.
- Jesus loves me unconditionally. The Father loves me unconditionally.
- Jesus is humble. The Father is humble.
- Jesus is good all the time. The Father is good all the time.
- Jesus always has UNHURRIED time for us. Father God always has UNHURRIED time for us.
- Jesus is never cruel or abusive. Father God is never cruel or abusive.
- We can talk to Jesus about our personal "stuff," and He will help us and not condemn us. In the same way, we can talk to the Father about our personal "stuff" without fear of condemnation, knowing that He wants to help us.
- With Jesus, we can fail and know that He still loves us just as much. With Father God, we have the freedom to fail, for He will also still love us just as much.
- Jesus never rejects us. The Father never rejects us.
- Jesus is forgiving and merciful. Father God is forgiving and merciful.

- Jesus' love for us is NOT performance-based. The Father's love for us is NOT performance-based.
- Jesus loves us, but hates sin because of what it does to others and us. In the same way, Father God loves us, but hates the sin that hurts us and hurts others.
- Jesus is always for us. The Father is always for us.

The list goes on and on. **The Father wants to have an intimate relationship with us. Yes, He is always worthy of our reverence and awe, but He also wants us to relate to Him as Daddy or Papa. Each one of us who is a born-again believer is one of His favorite kids!**

Chapter 7

OVERCOMING FEAR AND INSECURITY

We are members of the kingdom of faith, hope, and love, living in a world largely under the control, or at least influence, of the kingdom of darkness. To walk in victory in this world as citizens of the kingdom of light, we need to walk free from fear and insecurity. There are two kinds of fears we are confronted with—external and internal.

Combating External Fears

The Bible directive for dealing with these fears is "above all, taking the shield of faith with which you will be able to quench all the fiery darts of the wicked one" (Ephesians 6:16). External fears come at us from outside, by the evil one barraging our minds with negative thoughts, which if we buy into them will produce fear, anxiety, worry, and unbelief in us. These are fiery darts thrown at us directly by the evil one. External fears also come to us indirectly from the evil one through the world system in which we live. The news we see or read is studded with fear. Also, people around us who do not have faith live in a state of agitation and worry, and we can become affected and infected by their anxieties. Fiery darts of fear, anxiety, and worry bombard us from the world system daily! Medical science, while being very helpful in many ways, also can introduce into our lives more things to worry about. In the midst of all this, it is no small challenge to stay in faith on a daily basis!

The Bible also says that we are to "fight the good fight of faith" (1 Timothy 6:12). **Our chief defense against ALL the fiery darts of the evil one is the shield of faith.** How do we hold up and strengthen the shield of faith in our lives?

- "So then faith comes by hearing, and hearing by the word of God" (Romans 10:17). We need a regular diet of the Word of God. Our Bibles are the greatest source of nourishment for our faith. How strong do you think you would be physically if you had one meal a week? Why do we think we can be strong spiritually by hearing a biblical message once a week? It is good we hear one, and it benefits our faith, but we need more!

- Pray in the Holy Spirit regularly. "But you, beloved, building yourselves up on your most holy faith, praying in the Holy Spirit" (Jude 20). This is a Bible prescription for strengthening our faith.

- Fellowship regularly with others in the household of faith. A hot coal on its own soon will stop glowing brightly and become dull, but a hot coal surrounded by other hot coals will continue to glow brightly. In addition to church meetings, we can fellowship together in homes, in restaurants, by email, and on the phone—wherever and however we get together with those of faith.

- Choose to believe what the Bible says over and above what the world, the flesh, and the devil say. The Word of God is truth, Jesus is the truth in Person, and the Holy Spirit is the Spirit of truth. **Choose to believe**

God and His Word over every other thought and every other opinion! And follow through by acting on what God says.

- All of us face faith versus fear decisions in our everyday lives. Our choices in these either build into us a habit of faith, or a habit of fear. Use these as an opportunity to strengthen your faith and to establish a habit of faith in your life. Treat these everyday situations as part of God's training or boot camp to make you battle ready! Then when confronted with bigger things, or bigger battles, your faith will be in good working order!
- Choose to speak in faith, not fear, doubt, and unbelief. This is one way in which we can choose faith over fear in our daily lives. This is not always easy, but our tongue is like a rudder that sets the course of our lives. **See James 3:2-5.** For example, when we get up in the morning we have a choice to make: Will we go by our feelings and the circumstances that confront us, or will we go by what God says?

One of the best things we can do for ourselves is to start the day off with unhurried time with the Lord, for no matter how you or I may be feeling when we wake up, we will feel better after our time with Him. Don't make it a religious or strained time. Make a hot drink and chat with Him like you would with a friend. After all, He is your best friend! You may say that your life is too full to do that. If your life is that full, you can't afford not to spend this time with Him, for how will you make it through the day without Him? Many have come to realize that when we give the Lord the first part of our money, the rest of our finances are blessed. Don't ask me how it works, but it does! The same is true about time. I have found that when I give the Lord the first part of my day, the rest of my day goes better. It may be that I have fewer battles, or it may mean that when battles come, I am able to cope with them better—but it works! I also have more peace in my heart as I go through the day, and it is easier to keep up the shield of faith and trust Him.

Confronting Internal Fear and Insecurity

> There is no fear in love; but perfect love casts out fear, because fear involves torment. But he who fears has not been made perfect in love.
>
> 1 John 4:18

For many years, I tried to combat my inner fears and insecurities in the same way as external ones, but did not have much success. I did not understand why until quite recently. We all have inner fears and insecurities arising from what we have experienced in life, and from parents who may have passed onto us fears and insecurities that they themselves inherited. And over and above all that, we have grown up in a world that lives as though we are all orphans without a Father to take care of us. I believe it is this last area where most of our inner fears and anxieties come from, living life as orphans and having to fend for ourselves.

When Adam and Eve fell, they lost that relationship with the Father and had to live as fatherless orphans. Imagine the awful feeling of insecurity that they must have felt after living in the fellowship and provision of a loving Father? That same orphan spirit has continued down to the rest of us, and the dog-eat-dog world in which we live is in a perpetual state of inner insecurity as a direct result of the fall. Jesus came not only to save us, but also to restore us to living in the love and provision of the Father, where we feel secure and safe.

As mentioned in the previous chapter, many of us have not fully entered into a relationship with the Father. As a result, we still live like fatherless orphans, even though we are saved! Something very interesting has started to happen in my life since beginning to walk in an intimate relationship with Papa God (Daddy God). Those inner fears and inse-curities are beginning to disappear as they are replaced by the security of walking in the love of the Father. When we live life separate from that relationship, we feel abandoned and left to fend for ourselves in life, exposed and vulnerable, and we are tormented by inner fears and insecurities. **The more we live life as sons and daughters of the living God, walking in the security and loving care of an intimate relationship with a loving Father who has our best inter-ests at heart all the time, the more our fears evaporate and are cast out!**

I have discovered very recently that the inner fears and insecurities that have hindered me since childhood, and that have resisted my best efforts to come free from them, are starting to go! It is truly amazing. It does not mean that I am totally free from inner fear yet, but I am freer than I ever have been! And I am on a road of increasing freedom as I learn to walk more and more in the loving care of an intimate relationship with *my* heavenly Father!

Chapter 8

BECOMING A SPIRITUAL SOLDIER

For our fight is not against any physical enemy: it is against organizations and powers that are spiritual. We are up against the unseen power that controls this dark world, and spiritual agents from the very head-quarters of evil.

Ephesians 6:12 (J.B. Phillips)

As believers, much of our time and energy often is wasted in fighting the wrong battles. We get caught up in battles with people, circumstances, and issues when our real enemy is pulling the strings behind the scenes. Certainly, there are wicked people who align themselves with the forces of darkness, but they are simply being used as pawns by the evil one and, in most cases, don't realize it. And, yes, there are issues worth fighting for, but unless we first win the spiritual war, our best efforts are likely to be in vain. We have to win the spiritual battle before what is happening in the physical, natural realm will start to come right.

In our personal lives, we can gain victory over the spiritual forces opposing our households, for this is our turf, and we have spiritual authority under Jesus as our Lord to reign in our sphere. However, when it comes to a community, one solo Christian cannot really do that. It takes the team—the believers in that community—to collectively take spiritual authority over that community and oust the evil one. Then the spiritual climate over that community will change, and changes will start to take place in the natural, such as people becoming open to the gospel, the crime rate dropping, the community becoming a safer and better place to live, the material needs of the community starting to be met, etc. In a city, the same thing is true, except on an interchurch scale.

Personal Victory

> In conclusion be strong—not in yourselves but in the Lord, in the power of his boundless resource. Put on God's complete armour so that you can success-fully resist all the devil's methods of attack. For our fight is not against any physical enemy: it is against organizations and powers that are spiritual. We are up against the unseen power that controls this dark world, and spiritual agents from the very headquar-ters of evil. Therefore you must wear the whole armour of God that you may be able to resist evil in its day of power, and that even when you have fought to a standstill you may still stand your ground. Take your stand then with truth as your belt, righteousness your breastplate, the gospel of peace firmly on your feet, salvation as your helmet and in your hand the sword of the Spirit, the Word of God. Above all be sure you take faith as your shield, for it can quench every burning missile the enemy hurls at you. Pray at all times with every kind of spiritual prayer, keeping alert and persistent as you pray for all Christ's men and women.
>
> Ephesians 6:10-18 (J.B. Phillips)

Before we can be effective as soldiers in the wider body of Christ, we need to learn how to gain victory in our own lives. Let us take a closer look at what is involved in becoming a spiritual soldier by examining what Ephesians says about the spiritual conflict.

Be Strong in the Lord

This passage starts by telling us that we need to be strong in the Lord—our own strength will not cut it! This means that we need to be full of the Holy Spirit, who is the Comforter or Strengthener, in order to participate in this battle. One of the reasons why many believers fail in the spiritual fight is they attempt to do it without His empowering.

Secondly, we need to wear the armor of God, not our own natural defense mechanisms or weapons. And thirdly, we need to stand in our place and not back down or run. This is the hardest part of the spiritual conflict, and if we are to stand, we can only do so in His strength and His armor. Our own natural strength, abilities, and intellect will not cut it. It is a spiritual war, not a natural or physical one! Let us examine each piece of armor in turn.

- **The belt of truth.** Truth holds our lives together, just as a belt helps hold our clothing together. Imagine a soldier going into battle without a belt! In our everyday lives, imagine what would happen to our finances, for example, if our bank statements did not truthfully tell us how much money we have. Think about what happens to a relationship between two people when they lie to each other. It is not long before it disintegrates. What would happen if the doctor that we go to did not tell us the truth, or if the dentist did not tell us we needed a cavity fixed before it was too late? Or if we were given a wrong bus or train or airline schedule to plan our vacation? What about being sold a reliable used car that turns out to be a lemon? We have all experienced the aggravation, or worse, of not being told the truth. We rely heavily on truth to live our daily lives, even in natural things.

How much worse is it if we believe lies about spiritual and eternal things? The written Word of God, the Bible, is our complete reference for truth, and the more familiar we are with the Scriptures, the more easily we will detect the enemy's lies. Jesus, the living Word, is the truth in Person. Further, as believers, we have the Holy Spirit who is the Spirit of truth living within us. He will witness on the inside of us to the truth, and He will cause us to feel uneasy on the inside when something coming at us is not true. **We all need a regular feed on the Word of God and regular unhurried time with our Lord, who is truth, to keep the belt of truth firmly around our lives!**

• **The breastplate of righteousness**. The breastplate protects the main part of our body, including our hearts. Without this protection, we would not last very long in the battle. This is also true in spiritual warfare. The believer who tries to walk in self-righteousness is soon put out of commission! The only righteousness that will avail is the righteousness of Christ, not our own, and we have to count on His righteousness in two distinct ways.

Firstly, Jesus is our imputed righteousness, which means that when we receive Jesus and are born again, God credits us with the righteousness of Jesus in place of our own unrighteousness. "For He made Him who knew no sin to be sin for us, that we might become the righteousness of God in Him" (2 Corinthians 5:21). We are clothed with the robe of Jesus' righteousness, and that is how God sees us.

Secondly, God wants to impart the righteousness of Christ into us so that we actually become more and more righteous in the way we live and in our thoughts, motives, and desires. To put it another way, God wants to make us more and more like Christ from the inside out. "For whom He foreknew, He also predestined to be conformed to the image of His Son, that He might be the firstborn among many brethren" (Romans 8:29).

In spiritual warfare, when the world, the flesh, and the devil try to bring us under condemnation because of our shortcomings, our defense is simple. Jesus is our righteousness—we are not our own—so our shortcomings are irrelevant. We also need to walk righteously in our everyday lives because if we live in sin, we are in the territory of the evil one, and we will be defeated. That does not mean that we have to be perfect, for we are in the process all our lives of becoming more and more like Christ. **However, it does mean that we must walk in all the light we have and not backslide into our old lives!**

- **The gospel of peace.** This piece of armor is for our feet; in other words, for our walk through this life and our stand in the spiritual conflict. Firstly, we need to be assured that we have peace with God. We are assured of this in Romans 5:1, which says, "Therefore, having been justified by faith, we have peace with God through our Lord Jesus Christ." To stand in the spiritual conflict, we need to be convinced of this in the very core of our beings, for in knowing this, we will know that God is for us, and if God is for us, who can be against us? (Romans 8:31). When we are walking in the peace of God, we can have firm footing in a world that is shaking, rattling, and rolling. The evil one will do his best to try and rattle us and disturb us out of the peace of God, for then we will be much more easy to knock down. There is a connection between faith and peace, for if we really trust God, we will know peace.

You will keep him in perfect peace,
Whose mind is stayed on You,
Because he trusts in You.

Isaiah 26:3

If our focus is on the Lord instead of on the wind and the waves, we will have peace. If our focus is on the wind and the waves and not on the Lord, we will be rattled. There is also a connection between prayer and peace, for if we will pray instead of worry, the peace of God will guard our hearts and minds through Christ Jesus (Philippians 4:1). In other words, we will be in a fortress of peace! Another trap to avoid is strife. The flesh in us and in others will try to stir up strife. We must learn to choose our battles wisely so that we avoid a lot of needless strife with others. We have to learn to **respond in the Spirit** when someone comes at us in the flesh, for if we **react in the flesh**, strife will steal our peace. The peace of God truly is a place where we can be unshakable in Him.

- **The helmet of salvation.** This helmet is also described as "the hope of salvation" (1 Thessalonians 5:8). As believers, our hope is in our Lord and Savior, Jesus Christ, and not in the things of this world. We have a glorious and eternal future ahead of us because of Jesus! The world around us does not have this hope, so when the future looks uncertain and insecure, the unbeliever has nothing solid to hope in. I would hate to be an unbeliever in the times we are living in! There is hope available to unbelievers, but it can only be found in Christ and not in the things of this life. Jesus said the following words concerning the hope that we have when things start to look REALLY BAD in this world: "Now when these things begin to happen, look up and lift up your heads, because your redemption draws near" (Luke 21:28).

While our hope is not in the things of this world, and although we can expect battles and opposition, we can experience blessings as we walk through this life. We belong to and serve a good God, who loves us and has promised never to leave us or forsake us. He also has promised to provide for all of our need out of His riches in glory in Christ Jesus. His amazing goodness is described in the following Psalm.

Bless the Lord, O my soul;
And all that is within me, bless His holy name!
Bless the Lord, O my soul,
And forget not all His benefits:
Who forgives all your iniquities,
Who heals all your diseases,
Who redeems your life from destruction,
Who crowns you with lovingkindness, and tender
   mercies,
Who satisfies your mouth with good things,
So that your youth is renewed like the eagle's.

Psalm 103:1-5

- **The shield of faith.** We live in a world of conflict between two kingdoms, the kingdom of faith, hope, love, and light (truth), and the kingdom of fear, hopelessness, hate, and darkness (lies). As we approach the end of the age, the light is getting brighter and brighter for those who are following Christ and His kingdom, and darker and darker for those who are caught up in the kingdom of the evil one.

But the path of the just is like the shining sun, that shines ever brighter unto the perfect day. The way of the wicked is like darkness; they do not know what makes them stumble.

Proverbs 4:18-19

55

As the world around us grows more and more fearful, we need to grow in faith, for "this is the victory that has overcome the world—our faith" (1 John 5:4). The shield of faith protects us from ALL the burning missiles that the evil one throws at us. These are arrows of fear, doubt, unbelief, worry, and anxiety, which attack us through our minds. How do we hold up and use the shield of faith? Various ways were given in the previous chapter. The central purpose of all these is to get our focus off whatever is coming at us, and onto the Lord and what He says. **Our FOCUS is all-important.** Who or what is our focus?

Peter taught us a valuable lesson when he got out of the boat and began to walk on water. As long as his focus was on Jesus and on His word "Come," he was fine. But when his focus was on the stormy wind that was churning up the waves, he began to sink (Matthew 14:28-31). The evil one will come at us with thoughts—arrows—of fear, doubt, anxiety, etc., to get our focus off the Lord and His Word and onto the problems we are facing. The evil one also will use the words of others who are unbelieving to get our focus onto the problems and to sow words of unbelief, doubt, and fear into us.

It is a daily battle to keep our focus on the Lord and what He says, and off the wind and the waves of adverse circumstances and adverse words. As one good song says, **"Whose report will you believe? We will believe the report of the Lord."** It is not that we don't have problems or that we should pretend that they don't exist. Rather, it is that we should bring them to the Lord in prayer and cast the burden of them upon Him in faith. Then our focus must be on Him and on what He says and not on them. Our focus must not be on the problems, but on the problem Solver! **We can walk over the waves and through the wind of our problems, situations,**

and circumstances in victory IF we keep our eyes (our focus) on Jesus and on His Word!

• **The sword of the Spirit.** This is identified as the word of God. Jesus, when faced with temptation in the desert defeated the evil one with the word of God. He did not argue, debate or have a discussion; He simply quoted the word of God! The devil even tried at one point to use the word of God wrongly against Jesus but the Lord replied with the word of God rightly used and defeated the devil again. The word of God is not our sword, but rather the sword of the Holy Spirit who indwells us and enables us to rightly use it. When we use the word of God as led and inspired by the Spirit, the enemy is no match for us!

Clearly, the more familiar we are with the Bible, the more the Holy Spirit has to work within our lives. Putting it another way, the more we know the Bible, the bigger and longer the sword is that is available to us. A believer who is full of the Word of God and also full of the Holy Spirit is a mighty warrior in battle! We have no cause for pride in ourselves, for we are totally dependent on the Word and the Spirit in this warfare. Humility keeps us in that place of dependence on the Lord and keeps us in the flow of His grace and power, for "God resists the proud, but gives grace to the humble" (1 Peter 5:5).

The sword of the Spirit is an offensive weapon as well as a defensive one. "For though we walk in the flesh, we do not war according to the flesh. For the weapons of our warfare are not carnal but mighty in God for pulling down strongholds"

(2 Corinthians 10:3-4).

Are You a Prayer Warrior or a Worrier?

> Be anxious for nothing, but in everything by prayer
> and supplication, with thanksgiving, let your requests
> be made known to God; and the peace of God, which
> surpasses all understanding, will guard your hearts
> and minds through Christ Jesus.
>
> Philippians 4:6-7

This passage, along with Ephesians 6:18, is an exhorta-
tion to persevere in prayer. One of the famous poets wrote,
"More things are wrought by prayer than this world dreams
of." A true statement indeed! We can pray, or we can worry,
and I believe that most of us spend too little time praying,
which is why we spend too much time worrying! Prayer
is also an offensive and defensive weapon in this warfare.
**When we spend time in prayer, our hearts and minds
are guarded and defended by peace. In addition, when
we pray, we make the way for God to move and act,
resulting in the kingdom of God advancing in the lives
of others and in our lives, and the kingdom of darkness
being pushed back. Praise God!**

Chapter 9

ENTERING GOD'S REST

Trust in the Lord with all your heart, and lean not on your own understanding; in all your ways acknowledge Him, and He shall direct your paths.

Proverbs 3:5-6

Who is really in control in your life? In practice, who is really in charge? To the extent to which we genuinely surrender the controls of our lives to the Lord, we can know rest. When we surrender full control to Him, we trust Him with all of our hearts. While we are still in control or in partial control of our lives, we are saying that we trust ourselves and our own understanding more than we trust God! I believe that the reason for much of the manipulation and control that plagues our lives and the lives of others, and, in fact, much of the body of Christ, is a lack of surrender to God. When we have surrendered all to His control, we can rest from all manipulation and control!

I went through a season in my life not long ago when I progressively let go *all* of my plans. I am not talking about bad plans, but good plans, including plans to serve God, plans that I thought were very good! I spent seven years in college and learned to analyze everything and to lean heavily on my own understanding. It took about nine months for me to let go my very last good plan and to come out with a new master plan. **My new master plan is that I have no plans!** What a relief to let God be in charge!

It was only when I had let go ALL my plans that a huge weight fell off my shoulders. I discovered a new level of peace and rest. I am also experiencing an exhilarating new freedom. The weight of the world is no longer pressing down on me. I am walking daily with the plan Maker in His plans for my life, which He unfolds before me **one day at a time!** All I have to do—and it is not a burden, but a joy—is to walk in fellowship with Him each day, acknowledging His lordship—His control—over everything in my day. Then I simply trust Him and obey Him as best I can hear, knowing that He is in control. **My days have begun to sparkle with a new lease on life.** He makes things happen; I don't. He initiates; I don't. I just cooperate with His initiative in simple faith and obedience, and things happen!

God is amazing! Letting Him take over fully without reservations sets one free to truly walk in newness of life with Him. It also sets one free to experience His rest. The Bible says, "There remains therefore a rest for the people of God. For he who has entered His rest has himself also ceased from his works as God did from His" (Hebrews 4:9-10). In a very real way, we can rest from all our works—our self-effort and striving—and let God do His works in and through us. We can rest in what Jesus has done for us on the cross for our full salvation. We could not save ourselves. Once saved, we cannot live the Christian life victoriously in our own wisdom or strength. We don't have to. **God has given us His Holy Spirit to lead and guide us—to direct our path—and to empower us daily to walk according to the will and the Word of God,** "for it is God who works in you both to will and to do for His good pleasure" (Philippians 2:13).

Let us look at some specific areas in which most of us struggle to enter God's rest, namely, our time, our finances, and our lifestyles. Incidentally, our level of rest, or lack thereof, also has an effect on our health.

Entering God's Rest in Our Finances

Honor the Lord with your possessions, and with the firstfruits of all your increase; so your barns will be filled with plenty, and your vats will overflow with new wine.

Proverbs 3:9-10

If we will put God first in our finances by giving Him the first part, then He will bless the rest of our finances. The Bible calls it the tithe, and it is 10 percent. For a long time, it was a principle that I did not live by, as I heard much teaching on the subject that came across as legalistic, and I knew that I was no longer to live under the Old Testament Law system. Actually tithing took place in the Bible before the Law was instituted, but the way it was so often presented to me just came across as an imposed external law, not an internal thing of the heart, and it turned me off. Another struggle I had was that I felt that I could not afford to tithe. (I have learned since that I cannot afford not to!) At any rate, this was an area of my life that for many years was unresolved until one day a brother explained it to me in simple terms. If a farmer plants a crop, he has to plant enough seed to get as much crop as he needs to get. If he plants less, he will not get enough crops! It was so incredibly simple! Biblically, if we want enough seed to make it financially, we have to plant 10 percent of what we have. We don't have to do it—God will still love us, and we can still have a good personal relationship with Him. But if we don't tithe, our finances will suffer!

To cut a long story short, I decided to try it, and our family finances have done much better as a result. I still had to learn the discipline of a budget, for God promises to "supply all your need according to His riches in glory by Christ Jesus" (Philippians 4:19). **He does not promise to supply all of our greed, nor everything that the ads on TV tell us we need!** But I have found that in tithing, and in learning the discipline of a budget, I have entered God's rest and am far more able to trust Him with our finances. By simply obeying Him, I am placing the responsibility of our making it in His hands and out of mine, and letting Him have control. While I did not tithe, the controls of making it were in my hands, and that was not a place of rest!

Entering God's Rest Concerning Time

> But seek first the kingdom of God and His righteous-
> ness, and all these things shall be added to you.
> Matthew 6:33

Have you ever wondered why we live in such a hurried world, where there often does not seem to be enough time to fit in all we need to in a day, and we feel like we spend much of our lives running, trying to catch up? As believers, surely there must be a different and better way for us to live than that of the world around us. I believe that for many of us, one of the main reasons for our continual hurry is that we have not surrendered ALL of the controls of our lives to God as discussed earlier in this chapter. However, there is another major reason that can cause us to live in hurry and rush and not walk in rest when it comes to time.

Do we honor God with the first and best part of our time? I believe that if we will seek God first in our time, then He will provide us with all the time that we need! It sounds miraculous, doesn't it? Yet God has promised that if we will seek first His kingdom and His righteousness, what we need will be added to us, and that includes time! Just as putting God first in our finances is beneficial to our financial health, putting God first in the use of our time results in a more productive use of the rest of our time, AND He causes the rest of our time to work out better. In fact, we find that we have enough time in the day to accomplish, without hurry, **all He wants us to accomplish in the day**. That does not mean we have enough time to accomplish all that **we want** to accomplish in the day, or all **others want** us to accomplish, either. But if we are truly serving one Master, then we will find that we have sufficient time to accomplish fully and only what He wants us to in that day without living in a hurry.

For me, the best time of day is first thing in the morning, and I have found that spending this first part of the day with the Lord has a beneficial effect on the rest of my day. In fact, the tougher the day that lies before me, the more I need this time! When I don't start the day with the Lord, I seem to have less peace, get more easily rattled, and find it more difficult to handle the problems that come up. And who does not have problems to deal with? When I do start the day with Him, I have more inner peace, which makes me less hurried and more efficient in the use of time. Things somehow seem to go better as though the machinery of the day has been oiled, and it has been by the Lord. The problems that arise don't seem quite so daunting. My inner spirit man has been built up, and there is more rest on the inside of me.

If you already put God first in your time, but still find yourself living in a hurry, may I suggest sowing more of your time to Him? Get up a little earlier and spend a bit more time with Him. **Be unhurried.** God is not in a hurry, and He wants to have unhurried time with you. You may have a routine for your time with Him, and some routine is helpful, but don't be a slave to your routine. Allow room for spontaneity, and ask Him to be in charge of the time. Relax and have fellowship with Him. Make a hot drink if that helps! There are some good books on quiet times that can help you find what works for you.

If you don't already do it, I challenge you to try giving the best part of your day to the Lord, whenever that is, and see what happens. Don't be legalistic about it, as then it becomes bondage, but try to do it most days for about a month, and see what happens! I predict that after a while, you will not want to miss those times!

Entering God's Rest Through Simplifying Our Lifestyle

> Therefore we also, since we are surrounded by so great a cloud of witnesses, let us lay aside every weight, and the sin which so easily ensnares us, and let us run with endurance the race that is set before us, looking unto Jesus, the author and finisher of our faith . . . .
>
> Hebrews 12:1-2

Another reason why our lives can be hurried and we feel overloaded is because they have become too cluttered and complicated. In this passage, the Christian life is compared to a race—not a one hundred-yard dash, but a race requiring endurance, a long-distance race. Anyone running a race, and especially a long one, does not want to carry any extra weight or baggage. It is easy to understand why we should not let sin ensnare us on this race, but what often is not realized is that there are weights, which can be good things, that can hinder us. For example, there can be activities that in themselves are harmless and even good, but do they really help us in the race that we are called to run? If not, they are simply cluttering up our lives!

The same is true about possessions, and this is probably not a popular subject to bring up. In this culture, we have so much "stuff" that we can be weighed down by it. It takes money to buy, time and care to maintain, space to store (which means we need a bigger place to live in). Do we really need it all? Is it really helping us in our particular calling to be about the Master's business? And do we really need to be involved in every activity that we are involved in? There are many good activities, **but are they God's activities for our lives?**

In my own life, I have become increasingly ruthless about pruning out everything that makes for clutter and complication so that I can stay simple and stick with the essentials. That leaves me freer to walk each day without perpetual hurry. That does not mean that there should not be some time for fun and relaxation. We all need time to relax and unwind. There are simple ways to relax and have fun that do not cost an arm and a leg and do not require large amounts of time. We are all different, and the Lord is able to help each of us find ways to relax and have fun that work for us. God is a loving Father, not a slave driver!

A Brief Note About Health

There are many good books on the subject of health, and this subject is beyond the scope of this book. However, I believe that medical science has discovered that many ailments are stress-related and that too much stress is detrimental to our immune systems. Rest is the opposite of stress and is the antidote to it. Not only do we need enough physical sleep and rest, but we also need inner rest and peace. Learning to live in God's rest in the midst of an increasingly stressed-out world can only have a beneficial effect on our overall health.

In Conclusion

I heard a wonderful illustration that really says it all.
A man was given a large beautiful painting for his office. He
took it into his office, but could not find a really good space
to hang it. So he removed everything from his office and
hung the picture in the best place. Then he moved back into
the office what could be fitted in around the picture. The rest
was left out of his office! Should that not be a picture of our
lives when we receive Christ? Should we not give Him the
best and central place in them, and then fit the remainder of
our lives around Him? And should we not leave everything
else out that won't fit in with Him? God bless you!

Chapter 10

REAL RELATIONSHIPS

> Jesus said to him, "'You shall love the Lord your God with all your heart, with all your soul, and with all your mind.' This is the first and great commandment. And the second is like it: 'You shall love your neighbor as yourself.' On these two commandments hang all the Law and the Prophets."
>
> Matthew 22:37-40

This passage is a description of what the Law and the Prophets were all about. Christianity is primarily about relationships and not really about religion. The heart of the Bible, from Genesis to Revelation, is firstly about relationship with God, and then about relationships with one another.

In James 1:26-27, where religion is mentioned in connection with believers, it is linked to bridling one's tongue, a very relational issue, and to our treatment of widows and orphans, also a very relational matter. This passage also instructs us to keep ourselves unspotted from the world, which at first glance may appear to support the idea that Christianity is a religion. However, when the Lord talks about walking righteously, it is walking in the righteousness of Christ and not the righteousness of man. It is first and foremost righteousness of the heart and not the external righteousness that the Pharisees walked in. Paul, when he mentions religion, is not referring to Christianity!

The church, therefore, is not meant to be a religious organization, but a living, relational organism (body) made up of real people having real relationships with one another. It has some organization, to be sure, but not in the sense of a worldly company! Organization in the body of Christ is meant to serve the people, and not for the people to serve the organization! The people are to serve the Lord, and then one another. It is not meant to be a worldly organization where a few call all the shots and everyone serves them. **The church is to be a service organization where God calls all the shots, and where we all serve the Lord and one another in love.**

We all have different functions in the body of Christ, and we should honor those entrusted with leadership. Those in leadership also should treat those having other callings with honor because each position and place in the body of Christ is important, and each person is worthy of respect. According to Jesus' own words, being great in the kingdom of God is just the opposite of what the world calls great. Great in the world is being able to lord it over others and have them serve you. Great in His kingdom is being a servant! (Matthew 20:25-26) Now, how many of us really want to be leaders?

The church is composed of real people who are living stones (1 Peter 2:4-5), not physical bricks and stones. The church can meet in a magnificent cathedral, a home, or an open field, but it is the people that are the church, not the place where they meet! Having a church home is having a home firstly in our relationship with the Lord, and secondly being related in a real way with a group of fellow believers who love us and can be straight with us, and with whom we can have interdependent relationships. We can meet in the most magnificent building that man can build, attend meetings with thousands of people, and have NO church home. We can meet in a barn or a humble building or a home and have some real, honest, loving relationships with a group of people, and when we meet, have the presence of God flow. Now that is a church home!

In the times we are living in, when things are getting tough and could get a whole lot tougher, we need to stand together in love and support one another in the body of Christ. The building that we meet in cannot help us, nor can a multitude of superficial relationships on the level of "How is your dog? How is your cat? Its nice weather we are having," be of any help to us. We need REAL RELATIONSHIPS with at least a few other believers, where we can share honestly with one another, pray for one another, help one another, be honest in love with one another, and encourage one another.

> And let us consider one another in order to stir up love and good works, not forsaking the assembling of ourselves together, as is the manner of some, but exhorting one another, and so much the more as you see the Day approaching.
>
> Hebrews 10:24-25

This passage says NOTHING about where we are to meet, but just that we should meet regularly, like hot coals coming together for mutual support so that we can stay hot!

Why is it that traditionally, we have given so much emphasis to where we meet when the New Testament gives so little emphasis to it? When the woman at the well questioned Jesus about the right place to meet, He answered as follows:

> Jesus said to her, "Woman, believe Me, the hour is coming when you will neither on this mountain nor in Jerusalem, worship the Father. You worship what

you do not know; we know what we worship, for
salvation is of the Jews. But the hour is coming, and
now is, when the true worshippers will worship the
Father in spirit and truth; for the Father is seeking
such to worship Him. God is Spirit, and those who
worship Him must worship in spirit and truth."

John 4:21-24

God is looking for genuine, wholehearted worship,
which goes beyond our understanding and into the spiritual
realm, where we can commune and communicate with Him
who is Spirit! When we get our eyes off the visible and onto
the invisible God, we enter into real worship and are able
to experience real fellowship with Him and, as a result,
real fellowship with one another. **God is allowing us to be
shaken in this season so that our focus moves away from
the things we can see and onto the invisible God that we
cannot see and His eternal kingdom.**

If then you were raised with Christ, seek those things
which are above, where Christ is, sitting at the right
hand of God. Set your mind on things above, not on
things on the earth.

Colossians 3:1-2

If we continue to be preoccupied with natural things, we
will stay babes in Christ and will not be able to stand firm. If
we will learn to rely daily on the One that we cannot see, to
rely on His Word, to be led by His Spirit, and to look to Him
as our Source in all things, we will grow spiritually stronger
each day. As a result, we will be more able to stand firm in
faith and peace in a world that is shaking and insecure and
has no peace. **We also will have the joy of walking with the
Lord through this time and being used by Him to help
others put their trust in Him!**

70

Chapter 11

WALKING IN LOVE

There is no fear in love; but perfect love casts out fear, because fear involves torment. But he who fears has not been made perfect in love.

1 John 4:18

We are designed to live in an atmosphere of love — God's love! When Adam fell, the whole human race was cut off from an intimate and loving relationship with God, and no longer lived in an atmosphere of His love. God has always been love, and it was not God that changed. He still loved man just as much, but the rebellion of man had separated us from that atmosphere of love. Christ came to restore us into that intimate relationship with the Father, into His full acceptance of us in the beloved, and into the atmosphere of His love.

However, the evil one works overtime to accuse us and to try to make us walk in an atmosphere of condemnation with its resulting fear and guilt. He tries to get us to focus on our own righteousness, which is always flawed. So instead of resting in the finished work of the cross and walking in God's unchanging love, we walk in guilt and fear. Many believers can't quite believe that God accepts them unconditionally and fully **on the basis of what Jesus has done alone.** They are aware of their own shortcomings and get their eyes off Jesus and onto themselves. The evil one is quick to use this to his advantage.

God's acceptance of us is never based on what we are like or on what we have done, but on Jesus' blood and righteousness and on what He has done! If the enemy can get us focused on the wrong and shaky foundation of our own righteousness, we will always walk in guilt and fear toward God. If we stay focused on the fact that we are fully accepted in Jesus because of what He has done for us, we can enjoy living in the unconditional and unchanging love and acceptance of God. **This is what we are destined and designed to walk in!**

What the world calls love is performance-based, but God's love does not change from day to day based on our performance. If we read our Bibles and pray regularly, God does not love us more. If we don't, God does not love us less. Of course, it is to our great advantage to read our Bibles and pray regularly because we will grow in our relationship with the Lord and become stronger believers. If we don't, we will suffer from spiritual malnutrition. But God's love for us does not change. **We can rest and feel secure in His unchanging love!**

It is an interesting fact that what we walk in ourselves is what we will communicate and pass on to others. We cannot pass on the love of God to others unless we are living in it ourselves. We can say the right words and quote the right Bible verses, but if we are not walking in it, it will not communicate. An example of this is given in the following verses.

Then they went into Capernaum, and immediately on the Sabbath He entered the synagogue and taught. And they were astonished at His teaching, for He taught them as one having authority, and not as the scribes.

Mark 1:21-22

Verse 22 is a remarkable verse. The scribes (and the Pharisees) knew the Word of God better than anyone else in their day. Their teaching would have been scriptural, but it carried no authority. Why not? They knew the Word, studied it, quoted it, but it did not come across with authority. I believe that although it was in their heads, it had not changed their hearts. They were not walking in what they were talking about, but Jesus was!

The more that we walk in a performance-based way in our own lives, the more performance-based and conditional will be our acceptance of others. The more we rest in and walk in the unconditional love of God for us, the more we will minister that same unconditional love to others, supernaturally naturally.

Love and Ministry (Service)

Though I speak with the tongues of men and of angels, but have not love, I have become sounding brass or a clanging cymbal. And though I have the gift of prophecy, and understand all mysteries and all knowledge, and though I have all faith, so that I could remove mountains, but have not love, I am nothing. And though I bestow all my goods to feed the poor, and though I give my body to be burned, but have not love, it profits me nothing.

1 Corinthians 13:1-3

This passage **does not mean** that we don't need faith, or supernatural gifts of the Spirit, or to help those in need. But what it does mean is that without love, all our service is in vain. All Christian ministry is meant to be carried out in faith AND love. The heart of Christianity is relational, and without love, we are ministering in an impersonal, non-relational way. How many marriages would survive if we related to one another on the basis of law and not love? God is love, and in all that He does toward us, He is motivated by love. Even when He disciplines us, He does so out of love so that we may not continue down a destructive road. We are called in the same way to do all that we do in love. In the natural, that is impossible!

God is to be the Source of all we do, and Jesus makes it plain in John 15:5 that apart from Him we can do nothing. If we try to love in our own strength or natural love, we will soon run dry. It is only to the extent that we are plugged into the love of God in our own lives that we can be channels of His love to others. The Christian life is not meant to be a life of self-effort and strain, where we try to minister and love in our own strength. **He wants us to walk in a love relationship with Him and to let Him pour His love through us to others.**

Our Motives for Service Far Outweigh Our Performance

> For in Christ Jesus neither circumcision nor uncircumcision avails anything, but faith working through love.
>
> Galatians 5:6

Love and faith (trust) work together to produce fruit in the kingdom of God. God is bigger than all our mistakes, and if our hearts are right, God can teach us and train us. He can even cause our imperfect performance to bear fruit in His kingdom. If our heart motive is wrong, then no matter how good it looks to man, and no matter how technically perfect our performance, it will amount to nothing in His kingdom. If

God was only interested in a perfect performance, He could have made us all a bunch of perfect robots! But God wants sons and daughters, who of their own free will serve Him because they love Him, and reverence and respect Him. He wants a relationship with us of love and trust, not of slavery and fear. God is love, and as His children, He wants us to walk in His love and to be channels of His love to others. The world needs love, but not our own conditional, impure, and selfish "love." **The extent to which we are living in a love relationship with the Lord is the extent to which we will communicate His love to others.**

Chapter 12

THE LOCAL CHURCH

In the church, there is a restlessness, turbulence, discomfort, and even dissatisfaction with church life as we know it. What is going on in the body of Christ? My wife and I were having breakfast in a restaurant one morning when the Lord began to show me something about this. What the Lord showed me that morning was not the whole picture, for "we see through a glass darkly." Nor do I claim to be able to explain perfectly what I saw with all the theological I's dotted and the T's crossed correctly, but here it is:

"A baby is about to be born, and at the moment it is in the birth canal which is an extremely uncomfortable place. The bride of Christ is about to emerge from the present unholy mixture of real Christianity, tradition, religion, idolatry, and just general man-made 'stuff' that at the present time we call the church. A glorious bride is about to emerge and rise up out of the ashes of the old. As anyone, especially a mother, knows, the last part of a pregnancy is extremely uncomfortable. There just seems no way to get comfortable for very long. And the birth itself is not an easy thing for mother or child!

"Those believers who genuinely love Jesus first, and who are willing to move with the cloud and follow Him wherever He leads, no matter how uncomfortable, and no matter what the cost, will be a part of the emerging bride. Loyalties will be tested, for our loyalty to Him must come before every other loyalty! Those who cling to the old, who are not willing to leave their comfort zones, and who are not willing to move with the cloud and follow Him will not participate in the glorious destiny that God has for the end-time church. Will they still be saved? I don't know. I would like to think that they will in the long run, but at the very least, they will miss the mark and miss out on the best that God has for them."

I believe that God is shaking, or allowing to be shaken, church life as we have known it. **Change is in the air, and many believers are feeling a hunger for more, more of God and more in their church life.** A number have opted out of conventional church life and have started house groups. Others have moved from church to church looking for something more but not knowing exactly what to look for. Still others are clinging to their comfort zones and traditions, and doing their best to resist and avoid change at all costs. Like it or not, God is moving the church into a new season, and things are not going to stay the way they are! God wants to take us individually and collectively out of shallowness and immaturity and into deeper water with Him and on to spiritual maturity!

How do we fit into local church life in all of this? I would like to say there is an easy solution, but I don't think that there is one.

What I would like to do is first look at several wrong solutions—wrong roads—that we may be tempted to follow in this time of change, and then give some suggestions that may be helpful in fitting in a right way into local church life.

The first wrong road is to become a spiritual lone ranger. This is a very attractive road, especially if one has been hurt badly. My conviction is that there are times when we need to draw aside for a season, but we are not meant to withdraw permanently! I was badly hurt in a local church many years ago. The Lord used my wife to stand by me when several people were doing their best to try and tear me down from my position. It got so unpleasant that I quit and did not go anywhere for about three months. I had long quiet times instead of going to church and experienced healing and a clearer vision of what the Lord had for my life. After that, a local pastor who knew what had happened welcomed us into his church to just be there without placing any demands on us. I experienced further healing, and I don't think that man had any idea just how much his kindness meant.

When one is hurt, it is a great temptation to withdraw permanently. However, I have come to believe that while God most certainly does not send the hurts that come our way, He allows them. Consider what Joseph had to go through on his way to the throne. Consider what David had to experience from Saul on his way to the throne. God has a calling for us to fulfill in this life, and He is preparing us to reign with Jesus throughout all eternity. The sufferings that these men experienced were totally unjustified—they did not deserve it. But God allowed it and used it as part of their preparation to take their places on the throne. Consider the unjust suffering that our Lord had to experience to purchase our salvation! The lifestyle of a lone ranger is actually a lifestyle of self-preservation, not the way of the cross, and it **will not** take you into your destiny. Brother or sister, you are on your way to the throne. **Do not let the world, the flesh, or the devil keep you from fulfilling your destiny!**

Another wrong road is to become a pew sitter who basically stays in his or her comfort zone. If one is sitting week after week in a church and is not growing more like Jesus, and is not being used in some way to draw others to Christ or to help others grow in God, one is becoming lukewarm and backslidden. Jesus hates lukewarm! Sitting comfortably in a pew week after week is certainly not the way of the cross, either, and also will prevent you from reaching Christian maturity and from fulfilling your destiny!

So what is the right road? There are some basics that we need to accept in finding it.

- GOD IS MOVING! Change is in the air. We are entering into a new season in the body of Christ and in the world. Like it or not, things will not stay the same. If we don't move with God, He will not be able to use us in what He is doing in these days. There is no security in the past. **Our security is to move with God**, and therefore to "abide under the shadow of the Almighty" (Psalm 91:1).

- WE HAVE TO GET OUT OF OUR COMFORT ZONES TO STAY IN THE RIVER OF GOD! God is more interested in our growth than in our comfort, and we need to have the same attitude of heart and mind. God wants to move us out of the shallows and into the deeps, out of the milk stage (unless you are a new or young believer) and on to the meat. He wants to take us on to maturity and fruitfulness. In this time of storms and shaking, we will not be able to stand unless we have deep roots in God and an intimate relationship with Him. A little dab won't do you! Shallow roots and superficial, comfortable Christianity will not sustain us in the days ahead.

- UNDERSTAND that we need to be part of a local church to help us stand in these times and so that we can help others stand. **We need to love and support one another as never before, and this will become increasingly true as the end of the age approaches.**

What Kind of Building Is the Church?

> Now, therefore, you are no longer strangers and foreigners, but fellow citizens with the saints and members of the household of God, having been built on the foundation of the apostles and prophets, Jesus Christ Himself being the chief cornerstone, in whom the whole building, being fitted together, grows into a holy temple in the Lord, in whom you also are being built together for a dwelling place of God in the Spirit.
>
> Ephesians 2:19-22

When going down the road of building a building for the church to meet in, it is important to avoid going down the road of religion and tradition instead of the road of New Testament Christianity. Under the old covenant, the temple was a physical structure—a tent or a physical building. It was the place where a holy God met sinful man. In it a curtain or veil still separated God from man. In the temple were many things, including an altar and a "most holy place" (which we would call a sanctuary).

When Jesus died on the cross, the veil in the temple was torn apart from top to bottom, signifying that access was now freely available to all through Him. In the New Testament, the temple is no longer a physical structure of any kind. Because of the sacrifice of Jesus on the cross and the shedding of His blood, men's hearts can be cleansed, and relationship with God can be restored. A holy God can now live in the hearts of men by His Spirit. These additional Scriptures also describe the new spiritual temple that has now replaced the physical temple.

> Do you not know that you are the temple of God and that the Spirit of God dwells in you?
>
> 1 Corinthians 3:16

81

> Coming to Him as to a living stone, rejected indeed by men, but chosen by God and precious, you also, as living stones, are being built up a spiritual house, a holy priesthood, to offer up spiritual sacrifices acceptable to God through Jesus Christ. Therefore it is also contained in the Scripture, "Behold I lay in Zion a chief cornerstone, elect, precious, and he who believes on Him will by no means be put to shame."
>
> 1 Peter 2:4-6

As believers, we are individually and collectively the temple of God because He lives in us! There is a sanctuary in each of our hearts individually, and when we meet together to worship Him in Spirit and in truth, there is a sanctuary in our midst whether we are in a beautiful building, a home, a school hall, or an open field! The physical building is a convenient place for us to meet—a facility and no more. When we leave the building, the church leaves, and the sanctuary leaves with us. **The people are the church!**

Look for a Local Church Base, Not a Box

A local church should be a base where we are to "consider one another in order to stir up love and good works, not forsaking the assembling of ourselves together, as is the manner of some, but exhorting one another, and so much the more as you see the Day approaching" (Hebrews 10:25).

However, it should not be a box that prevents us from freely fellowshipping with other believers in different local churches. We also should be able to function in our callings both inside and outside our local churches. We are also called to be witnesses in the world outside the boundaries of our local churches! Jesus said, "I am the door. If anyone enters by Me, he will be saved, and will go in and out and find pasture" (John 10:9). When a local church becomes a box, where everything happens inside the box, our growth is stunted, our fruitfulness in the Lord's service severely reduced, and I believe that God is not pleased.

Conclusion

PRAY for the Lord's right local church for you, and be willing to explore. In your search, do not focus on externals, such as whether the church meets in a magnificent building, or a humble hall or a home. The church is about making Jesus our first love and preeminent loyalty. It's about real relationships with real people who are hungry for more of God, people who walk in love and base their lives on the Bible. And people who believe that all that the early church experienced is still available for us today. The church is about acknowledging that Jesus is Lord and having leadership that is not manipulative or controlling, but humble and willing to let God be in charge.

There are no perfect churches, just as there are no perfect Christians. If you find a perfect church and join it, it will no longer be perfect! We can either stand on the outside as spectators or critics, or we can take our places as imperfect people in imperfect local churches that God is in the process of perfecting. **God has not called us to be spectators or critics, but to be fellow members of the body of Christ in the most glorious season of opportunity for the church in all of history**. Do you want to be one of those who stands on the sidelines and misses the action at the end of the age? Or do you want to be a full participant in the end-time army of God? Yes, there are risks, and yes, you will make mistakes, but God sees our hearts, and **He is well able to use ordinary, willing people who love Him to do extraordinary things!**

God bless you.

Chapter 13

LIGHTS SHINING IN THE DARKNESS

But the path of the just is like the shining sun, that shines ever brighter unto the perfect day. The way of the wicked is like darkness; they do not know what makes them stumble.

Proverbs 4:18-19

As we travel down the road toward the end of the age, the light is getting brighter and brighter for those on the path of life, and darker and darker for those on the path of sin and death. The gray shades are fast-disappearing, and the days of being able to have one foot in Christ and one in the world are vanishing fast. As the shaking in the world continues and even intensifies, it will become increasingly difficult to straddle the fence and live a life of lukewarmness and compromise with the world. As believers, we are going to wind up as sold out for Christ, or turning our backs on Him and becoming lovers of this world system, following after "the lust of the flesh, the lust of the eyes, and the pride of life" (1 John 2:16).

One of the more disturbing trends in some parts of the body of Christ in recent years is the emphasis on material prosperity. Jesus said very plainly, "No one can serve two masters; for either he will hate the one and love the other, or else he will be loyal to the one and despise the other. You cannot serve God and mammon" (Matthew 6:24). Mammon represents the god of material prosperity. How, then, can we preach Christ and mammon? Certainly, the Lord has promised to "supply all your need according to His riches in glory by Christ Jesus" (Philippians 4:19). But it does not say He has promised to supply all of our greed.

Biblical prosperity is relational—it is a by-product of our relationship with the Lord, not a result of our seeking it. The material things that we need will not be added to us by seeking them, but by seeking Him! Jesus makes it very plain in Matthew 6:25-34 that we are not to spend our lives seeking our material needs like the Gentiles, meaning unbelievers. He says, "But seek first the kingdom of God and His righteousness, and all these things shall be added to you" (Matthew 6:33).

We can trust God to supply all that we need—He is the best Father! Very often He goes way beyond and gives us more than we need. However, our focus must be on the Lord, and our seeking must be reserved for Him alone; otherwise, we will fall into idolatry. We will then suffer the same consequences that Israel did in the Old Testament when she went into idolatry. **If we are to be lights shining for Jesus in an idolatrous society, we must be free from idolatry ourselves.**

Lighthouses

> You are the light of the world. A city that is set on a hill cannot be hidden. Nor do they light a lamp and put it under a basket, but on a lampstand, and it gives light to all who are in the house. Let your light so

shine before men, that they may see your good works
and glorify your Father in heaven.

Matthew 5:14-16

The Lord wants to shine through us with brightness and
intensity in these days. He is looking for people who are free
from mixed motives, people who are wholeheartedly devoted
to Him as their first love. He is looking for people who will
simply obey Him out of love, not out of the slavery of fear,
people who have laid down their own kingdoms and their
own agendas to be available to Him for the service of His
kingdom, and who will walk in His agenda for their lives.

The amazing thing is that when our lives are self-
serving, we do not find the fulfillment that we desire. Even
if we accomplish what we set out to do, it does not bring
us the peace, joy, and lasting fulfillment that we thought it
would. On the other hand, if we surrender our lives to Him
and allow Him to direct them according to His will, we experience living in fellowship with the One who satisfies our
deepest longings. We also start to experience the true fulfillment of walking in that for which we were created. **We find
ourselves walking in the freedom we were created to walk
in because we are doing what we were created to do!** God
loves us and knows far better than we do what will truly
fulfill us. And when our lives are surrendered to His will, we
also will become channels of His blessing to others.

Then Jesus said to His disciples, "If anyone desires
to come after Me, let Him deny himself, and take up
his cross and follow Me. For whoever desires to save
his life will lose it, but whoever loses his life for My
sake will find it."

Matthew 16:24-25

A lighthouse is built on a foundation so strong that no storm can knock it off. It also shines with brightness and intensity in the darkness so that it can be clearly seen, even from a distance. The Lord wants each of us to be like a lighthouse, built so firmly on Him that we will stand firmly in this season of shaking and by our lives will shine with brightness and intensity in the gathering gloom. The level of insecurity in the world around us will very likely continue and increase in the times in which we live, and He wants our lives to point many to Him as the only genuine and lasting security in this life and in the life to come.

Brother or sister, no matter what your age, the Lord wants to use you—**yes, you.** He wants to use you in a mighty way in these days! He wants to use you to draw unbelievers to Him and to encourage other believers who are struggling in their faith to stand firm in Him. It has nothing to do with how small or great you are in the eyes of others, or even in your own eyes. It has everything to do with your relationship with Him. **Strong Christians are not people who are strong in themselves, but those who have a strong relationship with Him.** As mentioned previously, His promise in John 15 is that if you abide—live, dwell, remain—in Him, you will bear fruit, more fruit, much fruit, and finally, fruit that remains! **Fear not. He who has called you can and will enable you to stand if you will habitually abide in Him!**

He who dwells in the secret place of the Most High
Shall abide under the shadow of the Almighty.
I will say of the Lord, "He is my refuge and my
    fortress;
My God, in Him I will trust."

Psalm 91:1-2

Chapter 14

A NEW SEASON

Do not remember the former things, nor consider the things of old. Behold, I will do a new thing, now it shall spring forth; shall you not know it? I will even make a road in the wilderness and rivers in the desert.

Isaiah 43:18-19

For the last year or two, I have been aware that we are entering a new season in the church as far as God's time clock is concerned. In the world around us, everything that can be shaken continues to be shaken. At the same time, there is a path of increasing light for believers to walk on (Proverbs 4:18). I have been aware of an increased level of spiritual warfare, and that the way we walked during the last season will be totally inadequate for this one. I believe that this new season will be more glorious by far than the last one! However, until recently, I have been like a blind man stumbling around in the dark, unable to describe the new season and not knowing how to walk in it.

Then the Lord turned the light on, and suddenly, I saw that Isaiah 35 is a perfect description of many aspects of the new season! It was so simple and so clear that I was amazed and am still amazed at this wonderful revelation.

The Cost of Entering This Season

A ship tied to the dock cannot embark on a new journey. In the same way, we can have ropes tying us to a dock in our lives. We all have in our pasts, in varying proportions, the good, the bad, and the ugly! These things can and do prevent us from moving forward with God. There are bad things that have happened, causing hurts that are still unhealed. Just pushing them under the rug won't work—we need to bring them to Jesus and ask Him to heal them. We need to forgive those who have hurt us, and that is not easy for those who have been badly hurt, but it is an essential part of the healing process. It is also essential if we are to move into the wonderful things God has for us in this new season. To be honest, the main reason I forgive people is for me, not them! I don't want what others have done to me in the past to mess up my life or my future!

The ugly things that we have done to others God forgives when we bring them to Him, for Jesus paid the price of ALL our sins. The devil will still try to make us feel guilty about the past, but he is a liar. When God forgives, He forgets, and there is no record of it in heaven!

What about the good things? Clinging to good things from the "good old days" can keep us from God's best. Also, clinging to good plans in the present can keep us from letting go of the ropes and moving forward with God. That is not to say that the plans we walked in during the old season were wrong for that season, but this is a new season!

One of the hardest things of all to let go of is our comfort zones. We feel safe and secure in our comfort zones. We have some measure of control there, and we know how to walk in them. But God is far more interested in our growth than in our comfort, and we will have to let go of the comfortable box or goldfish bowl that we live in and be willing to let God take us out into the open sea with Him! I **believe that an essential step to entering this new season is to abandon our plans, agendas, programs, and ambitions. Leave them on the dock and wave good-bye to all of them!** Then we will be free to enter into the fullness and newness that He has planned for us in this time.

DESCRIPTION OF THE NEW SEASON

Restoration

The wilderness and the wasteland shall be glad for them, and the desert shall rejoice and blossom as the rose; it shall blossom abundantly and rejoice, even with joy and singing. The glory of Lebanon shall be given to it, the excellence of Carmel and Sharon. They shall see the glory of the Lord, the excellency of our God.

Isaiah 35:1-2

The Lord wants to make the dry, barren, unfruitful, and even seemingly dead areas in our lives come to life! He wants these areas, and our lives in general, to bloom and blossom and become places where streams of living water flow. He wants to reignite our hearts with those promises that He gave us in the past and bring them to birth. This is a season of restoration and fulfillment of those promises that have not yet come to pass. This is a season of fruitfulness—a season of "exceedingly abundantly above all we can ask or think."

Battles and Deliverance

Strengthen the weak hands, and make firm the feeble knees. Say to those who are fearful-hearted, "Be strong, do not fear! Behold, your God will come with vengeance, with the recompense of God; He will come and save you."

Isaiah 35:3-4

We can expect more spiritual opposition in this season than in the last one, and that the battles will be more intense. The enemy will try to discourage us from entering into this season and once we are walking in it will try to oppose us from going forward in it. We are a threat to the enemy's kingdom. Every believer who walks in the fullness that God has planned will result in the pushing back of the kingdom of darkness and the expansion of the kingdom of light! **God is telling us in this passage that no matter how shaky we may feel, we MUST NOT QUIT! If we will hold our positions in faith, God will surely and mightily deliver us every time!**

Manifestations of the Kingdom

Then the eyes of the blind shall be opened, and the ears of the deaf shall be unstopped. Then the lame shall leap like a deer, and the tongue of the dumb sing. For waters shall burst forth in the wilderness, and streams in the desert. The parched ground shall become a pool, and the thirsty land springs of water; in the habitation of jackals, where each lay, there shall be grass with reeds and rushes.

Isaiah 35:5-7

When Jesus walked the earth, healings, deliverance, and the supernatural were a normal part of His ministry. They were demonstrations of the kingdom of God, which had the power to oust the evil one and his kingdom. The early church walked in the power of the kingdom of God, and signs were a normal part of the preaching of the gospel. "And they went out and preached everywhere, the Lord working with them and confirming the word through the accompanying signs. Amen" (Mark 16:20).

As we approach the end of the age, we can expect increasing manifestations of the kingdom of light and the kingdom of darkness. It is clear that the world around us today is seeing increasing manifestations of the evil kingdom. It is not surprising, therefore, that in this season, we will see the power of the kingdom of God increasingly released. The world will not only hear the truth preached, but will see the love and power of the kingdom of God demonstrated. In the West, we have experienced some of this, but in general, we have been slower to come into these manifestations of the kingdom than in many other parts of the world. However, for those who are willing to follow Jesus wherever He leads, I believe that we, too, will increasingly experience the supernatural power of God in operation. **Healings, deliverance, signs, and wonders will become a normal part of Christian life and witness in this season!** Praise God!

The Highway of Holiness

A highway shall be there, and a road, and it shall be called the Highway of Holiness. The unclean shall not pass over it, but it shall be for others. Whoever walks the road, although a fool, shall not go astray. No lion shall be there, nor shall any ravenous beast go up on it; it shall not be found there. But the redeemed of the Lord shall be there, and the ransomed of the Lord shall return, and come to Zion with singing, with everlasting joy on their heads. They shall obtain joy and gladness, and sorrow and sighing shall flee away.

Isaiah 35:8-10

There is a highway for us to walk on as believers. It is not the low ways of the world around us that will involve us in sin and take us into the territory of the evil one, where we will suffer real destruction. The Highway of Holiness is the King's highway, and no lion or ravenous beast can climb onto it. Lions and ravenous beasts represent evil spirits and demonic forces, and this highway is off limits to them, for it is the Lord's territory. It is a safe highway for us to travel on as we journey through life.

The evil one will do his best to try to tempt us or deceive us into leaving this road, for he knows that he cannot touch us on it. We have to know that, too, and to be aware of the serious consequences of leaving that road. The stakes are much higher now as we approach the end of the age, and the level of spiritual warfare is also great. Therefore, the consequences of leaving the Highway of Holiness will be far more disastrous for us, for our loved ones, and for the ministries that we have been called to. Temptations are all around us in great abundance in these days. **We cannot avoid temptations altogether, but we are safe as long as we don't yield to them and leave the King's highway!** And if we do get off it, we need to repent and get back on it ASAP, before further damage results. This is not a time to be found in the wrong place!

This highway is also a way of increasing joy and gladness. There has been an emphasis on praise and worship in recent years, and I believe that this will continue to be an increasing emphasis as we march on toward the end of the age. In the Old Testament, it was frequently those carrying out praise and worship that led the armies into victory (e.g., 2 Chronicles 20:21).

It is a highway where victories are won and "sorrow and sighing shall flee away" as we come into a closer and closer walk with the Lord. On this highway, we will experience more and more of His presence until one day,

He returns in glory, or we reach the end of our race and cross over into glory with Him! Hallelujah!

LaVergne, TN USA
16 July 2010
189777LV00003B/32/A